C000125321

Father

Introduction	*8*
Celebration of an Encounter	10
I Knew You Would Come Home	14
The Elder Son	22
Show Us the Father	28
Night Truly Blest!	32
Only Son Nearest to the Father's Heart	36
Lord, Teach Us to Pray	40
Where Even Two or Three Are Gathered in My Name	44
To Walk Humbly with Your God	46
I Have Carved You on the Palms of My Hands	50
Like a Weaned Child in His Mother's Arms	54
Make Your Home in Me	58

*T*he Return of the Prodigal Son was painted in 1669 by Rembrandt van Rijn, a native of Leyden in the Netherlands. It was probably one of the last paintings that he completed before his death. It is a very large painting *(244 x 183 cm)* and is hung in the Hermitage Gallery, St Petersburg.

The painting describes the return of the Prodigal Son in the parable that Jesus told and it is a powerful tribute to Rembrandt's own faith. It was painted at the end of a long life of suffering and many losses including that of his beloved wife, Saskia, and his only son, Titus, at the age of twenty-seven.

Show us the
Father

The Return of the Prodigal Son by Rembrandt

• Reflections • Prayer • Scripture

Magdalen Lawler

Pauline

BOOKS & MEDIA

First published in the United Kingdom as *In Celebration of an Encounter* in 1996

This edition published in the United Kingdom in 2012
Pauline Books & Media
Slough SL3 6BS

© 2012 Pauline Books & Media UK

Cover/book design MaryLouise Winters fsp

Scripture texts from the *Christian Community Bible*
© 1999 Bernardo Hurault, Claretian Publications. Used with permission.
Within the reflections some of the Scripture texts are excerpts from *The Jerusalem Bible*,
copyright © 1966 by Darton, Longman & Todd, Ltd and Doubleday, a division of Random House, Inc
Reprinted by Permission.

I knew you would come home – from the CD *Winter Gifting* and ***Where even two or three are gathered
in my name*** – from the CD *All Will Be Well* both by Tom McGuinness sj, used with permission.

ISBN 9781904785637

auline

BOOKS & MEDIA
Middle Green, Slough SL3 6BS – UK
0044 (0) 1753 577629
www.pauline-uk.org
email: marketing@pauline-uk.org

Pauline Books & Media is an expression of the ministry of the Daughters of St Paul,
an international Catholic community of religious women, dedicated to spreading the Good News of Jesus Christ.
In imitation of the Apostle Paul, who used every means to proclaim Christ, the sisters work with modern media
and technology for evangelisation.

We shall celebrate and have a feast…

About the author

Magdalen is a Sister of Notre Dame. She has degrees in Art, History of Art and in Theology. She is also a qualified teacher. After many years teaching art and religious education in secondary and tertiary education, Magdalen trained at St Beuno's in 1980 and was part of the retreat team at Loyola Hall, Merseyside, from 1980-83. Since then she has worked in retreats and spiritual direction in tandem with student chaplaincy at Liverpool Hope University and at Heythrop College, University of London. Now retired, Magdalen offers retreats throughout the UK. She has a special interest in women's spirituality and in the relationship between spirituality and the visual arts.

She is the author of **Encountering Christ – Conversations with Women in John's Gospel, Contemplating Christmas,***as well as* **Pathways to God's Goodness – the Spirituality of St Julie Billiart** *obtainable from www.sndden.org. Her most recent book is* **Christ, Our Morning Star**, *published by* **Pauline Books & Media**.

About the poems

The poems of Tom McGuinness, with his own introductions, are a prayerful accompaniment to Jesus' beautiful parable of homecoming celebrated in this reflection booklet. These poems are available in song on two CDs: **Winter Gifting** *and* **All Will Be Well**.

In his own words

I knew you would come home was originally written when I was thinking about those who long for the return of a partner or child from war or conflict abroad. When I sing it I see the faces of those distant from home as refugees or asylum seekers. Perhaps these words may also remind us of those longing to speak again to a son or daughter who has suddenly left home. I tried to express the intensity of such longing with the phrase: **Somehow my heart could see you**. This song echoes the deep longing of God to hold us safe and welcome, free from loneliness and fear.

It is difficult to hold on to such hope in our fragmented world, but the song **Where even two or three are gathered** is a reminder of Jesus' prayer about the reign or living community of a loving God. This is a kingdom not made with power or wealth but with the certain hope that our strength is in the care and support we give each other. Whenever we gather together in mind and heart, sharing the bread of our lives, we are promised that God is truly there among us.

Tom McGuinness sj

Celebration of an encounter

The theme of Rembrandt's painting represents the spiritual homecoming of all humankind. It shows the Prodigal Son being welcomed back by his father. To one side, according to some experts, the elder brother looks on and in the background are other unknown figures who, like ourselves, contemplate the scene.

Take some time now simply to enjoy the colours and shapes in this painting.

Rembrandt uses a very limited palette of deep browns, ochre and white, but these are imbued with internal warmth which issues from the vibrant and evocative reds and the warm, golden tints. Throughout his life, Rembrandt pursued the mystery of light. In this picture he mingles light and darkness in a way that suggests a rising dawn, a burst of sunlight, a glowing hearth, or more deeply, the mystery of a resurrection-picture already unfolding before our gaze.

The central figures of the father and son form a glowing focus. The picture resembles a vaulted archway, lit from within, or a burning candle, held aloft to attract our attention to the mysterious drama being played out before our eyes. With a gentle, bending, gesture of love, the father welcomes back his son.

Subtlety is the keynote to Rembrandt's technique and the guide to understanding his image of God. This is a God who always takes the first initiative, who stoops to us, gently beckoning and holding us close. We need only to have the insight to recognise the home to which we truly belong.

Julian of Norwich has a wonderful phrase in her *Showings*, in which she describes God as 'the astonishing familiarity of home', a phrase very close to Jesus' own words when he says, 'Make your home in me as I make mine in you' *(Jn 15:4).*

As you enter into the contemplation of this picture in your prayer, consider which person you identify with most closely. See how you feel about each character. Which one most resembles your own feelings at this time?

Simply be aware of this and gently present those feelings to a God who paints and creates us on the great canvas of life, lovingly mixing our colours and applying brush strokes now with great delicacy and then again with exuberance as we emerge from the darkness of indecision and fear into the light of love and acceptance.

prayer – the light of the world

☐ Take one or more candles and place them in the centre of the group and close to the painting. Try to use candles in harmony with the colours of the painting.

☐ Focus on the figures of the father and the son. Remain in silence for a while. Then share what struck you most about the colours of this painting and what thoughts you had about the father and son.

☐ We call Jesus the Light of the World and Christian painters often help us to understand this truth by their clever use of light. Use one of the following scripture passages to share your prayer about how Jesus brings light into your life.

scripture

•• *God saw that the light was good and he separated the light from the darkness.* •• (GN 1:4)

•• *Lord, you are a lamp for my steps. My God, you brighten my darkness.* •• (Ps 18:28)

•• *Light that shines in the dark: light that darkness could not overcome.* •• (JN 1:5)

•• *Jesus spoke to them again, 'I am the Light of the world; the one who follows me will not walk in darkness, but will have light and life.'* •• (JN 8:12)

•• *As long as I am in the world, I am the light of the world.* •• (JN 9:5)

I knew you would come home

Read the gospel account of the Prodigal Son and try to imagine the father. Watch the scene of the encounter between father and son.

●● *There was a man with two sons. The younger said to his father, 'Give me my share of the estate.' So the father divided his property between them.*

Some days later, the younger son gathered all his belongings and started off for a distant land where he squandered his wealth in loose living. Having spent everything, he was hard pressed when a severe famine broke out in that land. So he hired himself out to a well-to-do citizen of that place and was sent to work on a pig farm. So famished was he that he longed to fill his stomach even with the food given to the pigs, but no one offered him anything.

Finally coming to his senses, he said, 'How many of my father's hired workers have food to spare, and here I am starving to death! I will get up and go back to my father and say to him: father, I have sinned against heaven and before you. I no longer deserve to be called your son. Treat me then as one of your hired servants.' With that thought in mind he set off for his father's house.

He was still a long way off when his father caught sight of him. His father was so deeply moved with compassion that he ran out to meet him, threw his arms around his neck and kissed him. The son said, father, I have sinned against heaven and before you. I no longer deserve to be called your son.'

But the father turned to his servants, 'Quick! Bring out the finest robe and put it on him. Put a ring on his finger and sandals on his feet. Take the fattened calf

and kill it. We shall celebrate and have a feast, for this son of mine was dead and has come back to life. He was lost and is found.' And the celebration began.

Meanwhile, the elder son had been working in the fields. As he returned and was near the house, he heard the sound of music and dancing. He called one of the servants and asked what it was all about. The servant answered, 'Your brother has come home safe and sound, and your father is so happy about it that he has ordered this celebration and killed the fattened calf.'

The elder son became angry and refused to go in. His father came out and pleaded with him. The indignant son said, 'Look, I have slaved for you all these years. Never have I disobeyed your orders. Yet you have never given me even a young goat to celebrate with my friends. Then when this son of yours returns after squandering your property with loose women, you kill the fattened calf for him.'

The father said: 'My son, you are always with me, and everything I have is yours. But this brother of yours was dead, and has come back to life. He was lost and is found.' ●● (Lκ 15:11-32)

As we look more closely at the painting, we notice the details of the central group more clearly.

The younger son is in an attitude of complete peace and rest on the bosom of his father, like a ship in harbour after a severe storm, or a sleeping child at its mother's breast.

The son's garments are tattered and torn like the sails of a ship that has battled with the ocean winds and currents. His sackcloth lies in deep and dark folds around his legs as darkness still clings to his being, which is only just unfolding in light. 'God is light and in him there is no darkness' *(1 Jn 1:5)*. The young man's head is shaven, like that of a convict or one who has been afflicted with lice or disease. His flesh is bruised, his sandals broken, as they hang, useless, one discarded in the dust.

The son is oblivious of the bystanders' stares, aware only of the presence of his father and the feeble heartbeat of the elderly man who holds him to his breast with a gesture of the hands unequalled in any other painting.

He is able to sense his father's special fragrance and the richness of his garments.

His eyes are closed to savour this intimate time of mutual love.

The two figures form one shaft of glowing light and their breath is mingled as their hearts beat in unison in the tent of meeting *(Gn 18:1-15)* which Rembrandt has created out of a roof of crimson and columns of pure gold.

prayer – with the imagination

Many of the mystical and spiritual writers as well as the authors of Scripture were familiar with the reality of our interior senses, recognising that sight, hearing, taste and smell all have parallels in our hearts. Interiorly we sense the touch of God and savour the mystery of One who dwells in light inaccessible, and yet is equally present in the love between a parent and child.

As we try to imagine what the father and son might say to one another, watch the scene. We can sometimes hear what the characters might say to us, too. Try to imagine yourself in their presence and watch the scene as it unfolds, looking around you at the other characters, observing their reactions. Do you identify with any of them? When you are tired of looking, simply rest in the peace that is to be seen on the face of the son.

scripture

Read John's first letter: 1:1-4

•• *This is what has been from the beginning, and what we have heard and have seen with our own eyes, what we have looked at and touched with our hands, I mean the Word who is Life…*

The Life made itself known, we have seen Eternal Life and we bear witness, and we are telling you of it. It was with the Father and made itself known to us.

So we tell you what we have seen and heard; that you may be in fellowship with us, and with the Father and with his Son, Jesus Christ.

And we write this to you that our joy may be complete. •• *(1 Jn 1:1-4)*

Read Luke 15:20 again and try to picture that moment.

●● *He was still a long way off when his father caught sight of him. His father was so deeply moved with compassion that he ran out to meet him, threw his arms around his neck and kissed him.* ●● *(LK 15:20)*

Rest and be at peace as you prayerfully reflect on the following passages:

●● *Thus says the LORD…*
Do not be afraid, for I have redeemed you;
I have called you by your name; you are mine.
When you pass through the waters, I will be with you.
When you pass through the rivers; they will not sweep over you.
When you walk through fire, you will not be burned;
neither will the flames consume you.
For I am your Saviour, I, the LORD, your God, the Holy One of Israel…
Since you are precious in my sight, and honoured–
Do not be afraid, for I have loved you… ●● *(IS 43:1-5)*

●● *Peace be with you; I leave you my peace.*
Not as the world gives peace do I give it to you.
Do not be troubled; do not be afraid. ●● *(JN 14:27)*

Prolong prayer by a meditative listening to the song.

I knew you would come home

I have dreamt so long that we would meet again,
I never doubted you, I knew you would return.
I have longed to see the moment you would come to me
through an open door bearing all the love we've known.
Oh I trusted you, I loved you so,
I hoped in you, I knew you would come home.

And, Oh I believed you were here:
sometimes my heart could see you!
Oh I believed in you,
somehow could sense you near me.
I have longed to say so many things to comfort you,
to hold you safe and welcome in my arms.
In the long and silent moment when the stars appear,
to speak the love which keeps you from all harm,
and gathers you and holds you still, guarding you from fear
while the loneliness and darkness disappear.

And Oh, I have called in my heart for you,
searching this lonely time,
wanting to tell you that even in darkness our love has grown.
And Oh, I believed you were here,
sometimes my heart could see you!
Oh, I believed in you somehow could sense you near me.

I trusted you, I loved you so.
I hoped in you, I knew you would come home.
I trusted you, I knew you would come home.

Tom McGuinness sj

21

The elder son

Standing in the background is the elder son
who also represents each of us. Less confident,
and suspicious of such a prodigal love displayed by his ageing father,
he hesitates on the verge of the action.

Yet his cloak reflects the colours of the central group
and he borrows dignity and confidence from their glowing unity.

He hovers at the edge of the light and absorbs it
almost involuntarily.

Maybe you understand how he feels
and would want to express sorrow for past resentments.

Perhaps you would like to absorb more of Jesus' light
into your own life.

Sometimes we find it hard to rejoice when others are fortunate
and we envy their good fortune.

Bitterness can result which needs the healing touch of the father
in the same way as the younger son needed it.

prayer – sorrow for our failings

You may wish to read the parable of the Prodigal Son again (Lk 15:11-32 on pages 14-15) and try to imagine the scene. Look at the elder son and the other characters.

How do you feel about the welcome that is being shown to the younger son?

Perhaps the elder son can help us as we try to come to terms with an image of a God who resembles an ageing parent, moved to tears by the return of a migrant son or daughter who has come to give comfort and strength for the final journey from this life. That God may rely on us for strength and comfort may be a new concept to consider.

scripture – forgiveness

Read and reflect on the correlation between love and forgiveness in the account of Jesus at the home of the Pharisee:

●● *'I tell you, her sins, her many sins, are forgiven, because of her great love. But the one who is forgiven little, has little love.'*

Then Jesus said to the woman, 'Your sins are forgiven.' The others sitting with him at the table began to wonder, 'Now this man claims to forgive sins!' But Jesus again spoke to the woman, 'Your faith has saved you; go in peace.' ●●
(Lk 7:47-50)

Read and reflect on the account of Peter's denial and the loving gaze of the Lord:

●● *Again Peter denied him with these words: 'My friend, I don't know what you are talking about.' He had not finished saying this when a cock crowed. The Lord turned around and looked at Peter and he remembered the word that the Lord had spoken, 'Before the cock crows today you will have denied me three times.' Peter went outside, weeping bitterly.* ●● *(Lk 22:60-62)*

Consider the Lord's response to Peter's question about forgiveness:

●● *If he offends you seven times in a day but says to you seven times 'I'm sorry,' forgive.* ●● *(Lk 17:4)*

scripture – images of God

Listen to your heart as you read the passages and stay with whatever touches you…

●● *Can a woman forget the baby at her breast and have no compassion on the child of her womb? Yet though she forgets, I will never forget you. See, I have written your name upon the palm of my hands.* ●● *(Is 49:15-16)*

●● *I have quieted and stilled my soul like a weaned child on its mother's lap; like a contented child is my soul.* ●● *(Ps 131:2)*

●● *I love you, O Lord, my strength. The Lord is my rock, my fortress, my deliverer and my God. He is the rock in whom I take refuge. He is my shield, my powerful saviour, my stronghold. I call on the Lord who is worthy of praise: he saves me from my enemies!* ●● *(Ps 18:1-3)*

●● *Clothed in majesty and splendor; O Lord, my God, how great you are!*
You are wrapped in light as with a garment;
you stretch out the heavens like a tent,
you build your upperrooms above the waters.

You make the clouds your chariot and ride on the wings of the wind;
you make the winds your messengers, and fire and flame your ministers.

You set the earth on its foundations, and never will it be shaken. ●●
(Ps 104:1-5)

...perhaps
   you would like to absorb
   more of Jesus' light
   into your own life...

Show us the Father

Our contemplation is now focused on that paternal figure – the father, the one whose love is without condition. Rembrandt's own preoccupation with old age and its wisdom, born of experience and suffering, has caused him to portray the father as an elderly man whose eyes are damp with sadness. His face is furrowed by years of searching for the son who is the beloved of his heart and the joy of his declining years. Focus on the parent-God who embodies all the qualities of tenderness and strength that we associate with those who have given us life and cared for us *(cf Jn 14:8)*.

How gentle is this old man of the Jewish ghetto! Rembrandt had contacts among Amsterdam's Jewish community. He recognised them as the people of the Bible and gave them an equal respect that was uncommon in his day. He loved to draw them and did what no other painter had done so well. Painting Jewish characters in Jewish dress, he reminds us that all the Bible stories had Hebrew origins and that Jesus himself was a Jew. In fact, he is the first artist to present us with a Jewish Christ.

This tender old man is the figure of an Israelite patriarch. The matriarchs and patriarchs of ancient Israel were those who followed a God, gradually being revealed to them, in wisdom and compassion as well as in might and justice. His bleary eyes symbolise the love that turns a blind eye to our failings. Their tired gaze has eagerly sought us. The richness of the old man's dress and his velvet yarmulke denote the richness of the grace which he dispenses as well as the material richness of the welcome he extended to the younger son.

prayer

You may like to invite someone from the Jewish community to speak to you about Jewish prayer and customs and the love of the Law (Torah). Read Psalm 119 about love of the Law.

Many modern instances help us to understand this picture. Young people flock to major cities, whether London or New York, for work and a new beginning. Sometimes they struggle to find employment and, harder still, accommodation. When they fail to obtain it, they feel they have disappointed their parents and they sometimes lose touch with home. Perhaps they turn to drugs and are exploited in their need. The father's face can remind us of parents we may have come upon in any modern city – mothers who search the streets, hoping to catch a glimpse of their daughters or sons – fathers who check among the homeless beneath bridges, longing to recognise a familiar profile or to be called 'Dad' again. Even when they fail to make contact, their search never ceases. They fear the rap at the door which might bring bad news, and at the same time they long for the hope that news might bring.

Arrange a prayer service with help from a local housing charity or refuge. There are many agencies that supply information about homeless young people. You may find a way to meet and help some of them in your city.

scripture

Listen to your heart as you read the passages and stay with whatever touches you.

●● *The LORD is gracious and merciful, abounding in love and slow to anger...*

  He does not treat us according to our sins, nor does he punish us as we deserve. ●● *(Ps 103:8,10)*

●● *No one has ever seen God, but the Only Son, nearest to the heart, has made him known: the one who is in and with the Father.* ●● *(Jn 1:18)*

●● *God so loved the world that he gave his only Son that whoever believes in him may not be lost, but may have eternal life. God did not send the Son into the world to condemn the world; instead, through him the world is to be saved. Whoever believes in him will not be condemned.* ●● *(Jn 3:16-18)*

●● *Philip said, "Lord, show us the Father and that is enough." Jesus said to him, "What! I have been with you so long and you still do not know me, Philip? Whoever sees me sees the Father; how can you say: 'Show us the Father'? Do you not believe that I am in the Father and the Father is in me?* ●● *(Jn 14:8-10)*

Night truly blest

The young man in the painting could almost be one of the homeless that we considered in our previous meditation. Sadly his like is to be seen all over the world. The young and vulnerable creep into alleys and entrances when night falls and the cold begins to bite. Night-time always accentuates Rembrandt's message and here he prepares us for one of the most profound understandings of night. It was only when night had fallen that the powers of darkness dared to challenge the power of Christ. *(Jn 13:30).*

Yet the risen Christ is to be encountered amid the tombs at the dawning of a new day. At the moment when the faint thread of dawn divides the most profound darkness, night and day are reversed. Night shines forth with splendour. It is truly blest, and more lovely than the dawn *(Easter Exsultet).*

The two central figures in the painting are surrounded by night, the night in which the younger son has lived for most of his short adulthood. A twilight hovers around the edges of the figures. Other characters can be traced in the shadows. Maybe they are part of the scene. Maybe they are simply bystanders who contemplate this mystery in our company: the light of God's eternal day dawns and a new creation for the son and for each one of us is realised.

It is in this setting that we begin to realise that Jesus himself is the only one who can effectively bring humanity back to the Father. There is a sense in which Jesus may almost be telling us the Prodigal story about himself. Although he could never have wasted the Father's substance, St Paul tells us that Christ Jesus was prepared to lay aside his divinity, 'assuming the condition of a slave' *(Phil 2:6).*

When we look again at the youthful figure that Rembrandt has painted, we see the sack-cloth of subjugation; the basic garment of humanity representing all the miseries of our world: famine, war, exploitation and human trafficking. The prophet Isaiah described the Lord's servant as 'a man to make people screen their faces; he was despised and we took no account of him' *(Is 53)*.

This is the sort of night and the kind of darkness that Jesus overcomes. Julian of Norwich, writing more than three hundred years before this picture was painted, seems to have had a wonderful insight into this truth. She might almost have painted this picture herself! 'Adam's old tunic, tight-fitting, threadbare and short, was then made lovely by our Saviour, new, white and bright and forever clean, wide and ample, fairer and richer, [even] than the clothing I saw on the Father' *(Shewings, Long Text ch 51).*

prayer

There must be many instances of deepest night which invade your own memory as you come to prayer. Ask for a more profound understanding of Jesus' humanity.

He entered our human experience in every detail so that he might identify with even the most degrading aspects of our existence and the disasters we bring about by our selfishness and greed.

scripture

●● *Jesus spoke to them again, "I am the Light of the world; the one who follows me will not walk in darkness, but will have light and life."* ●● *(JN 8:12)*

●● *Judas left as soon as he had eaten the bread. Night had fallen.* ●● *(JN 13:30)*

●● *To him, alone immortal, who lives in unapproachable light and whom no one has ever seen or can see, to him be honour and power for ever and ever. Amen!* ●● *(1 TIM 6:16)*

●● *The Lord is spirit, and where the Spirit of the Lord is, there is freedom. So, with unveiled faces, like mirrors, we all reflect the Glory of the Lord, while we are transformed into his likeness and experience his Glory more and more by the action of the Lord who is spirit.* ●● *(2 COR 3:17-18)*

●● *God is light, in whom there is no darkness.* ●● *(1 JN 1:5)*

Only Son
nearest to the Father's heart

As we now understand what is, perhaps, the most profound meaning of the painting, we remember the words at the beginning of John's gospel: 'No one has ever seen God; it is the only Son, nearest to the Father's heart, who has made him known.' *(Jn 1:18).*

Rembrandt presents, for our contemplation, the relationship that is possible between humanity and God.

At the heart-centre of the father and son's embrace is a heart shape indeed. Formed by the head of the son in the hollow of his father's breast, it is almost impossible to tell where one living figure ends and the other begins. The chiaroscuro of that space blurs the edges between humanity and divinity so that we do not know, except in our own hearts, where either begins or ends, or indeed, where we ourselves begin or end, except in God. A cave is created, like the one into which Elijah crept when he sought the face of God and was astonished to discover it in a gentle, whispering breeze. A womb-space is evoked in which God gives birth to a new child of the Spirit, labouring ceaselessly in creation until she can look on the face of her child. The child lies, newly born, on the heart of the mother, and is already free and wise beyond his years. These are the images which the heart of God may call forth. Jesus listens to the secrets of the heart of God in a gesture which bespeaks his unique intimacy. It is Jesus who literally shows us how the heart of God beats. 'I tell you solemnly, the Son can do nothing by himself. He can only do what he sees the Father doing' *(Jn 5:19).*

The expression on the face of the son is one of complete peace. The peace that surpasses understanding is here revealed before our wondering gaze. The customary Jewish greeting, *Shalom*, is transformed into the hallmark of perfect accord between God and humanity. 'A peace the world cannot give, this is my gift to you' *(Jn 14:27).* Jesus made it possible for us to be as close to God as he is. His home is our home. The place where Jesus dwells is always nearest to the Father's heart.

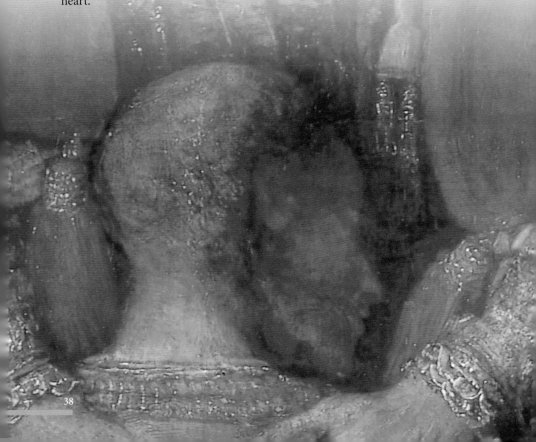

prayer – of the heart

Possibly this period of prayer can only be approached in the sort of contemplative manner that many writers call 'stillness' or 'centring prayer'.

A helpful way of praying for some people is to just sit quietly.

As you breathe in, be aware of breathing God's life into your heart through Jesus.

As you breathe out, offer back to God the hopes and prayers of your own heart. 'Whoever believes is a child of God' (1JN 5:1).

scripture

On that day you will know that I am in the Father and you in me and I in you. Whoever keeps my commandments is the one who loves me: and whoever loves me will be loved by my Father, and I shall love him and reveal myself to him.' (JN 14:20-21)

40

Lord, teach us to pray

As we grow to understand that the place where Jesus continually dwells is that intimate place nearest to the heart of God, it is to him that we turn in order to learn how to pray. The gospels tell us that Jesus spent time in intimate communion with God; time and space where he could be alone with God.

Mark tells us that, 'Early in the morning, long before dawn, Jesus got up and left the house and went off to a lonely place and prayed there' *(Mk 1:35)*. The house that Jesus left was Simon's house, where the previous day he had cured Simon Peter's mother-in-law. As a result, that evening the whole town came crowding around the door and he cured them until late in the day. So, in the morning he needed that centring space that we all need if we are to reflect on our relationship with God. At different times in our lives, God will be revealed to us in different ways. As we mature we draw nearer to an adult understanding of God.

Matthew also tells us that at the end of another tiring day, Jesus withdrew to be alone with God. This time it was in the evening after the feeding of the crowd who had followed him around the lakeshore of the Sea of Galilee. 'After sending the crowds away, Jesus went up into the hills by himself, to pray. And when evening came, he was there alone' *(Mt 14:23)*.

We all know how difficult it is to find space in our increasingly busy urban lives. Focussing can help us to be aware of God. Perhaps we live on the fifth floor of a building, on the tree-line. Watching the changes of the seasons and seeing the wind stirring in the tree can give us a focus that will slow us down and help us to be aware of God's presence in our lives. Listening to a favourite piece of music, tending a window box, or simply switching off for five minutes during a lunch break and deliberately slowing down as we sip our coffee or green tea can not only remind us that God awaits us but it can also be good for our physical health. Websites like *pray-as-you-go.org* or *sacredspace.ie* exist to help people to pray in the midst of a busy life. Many religious congregations also offer suggestions for prayer on their own websites.

*...at different times in our lives,
God will be revealed to us in different ways...*

scripture / prayer – Jesus' teaching

This prayer to the Father in Jesus' own words is the prayer that unites all Christians. Each line brings us closer to an understanding of the story of the Prodigal Son.

•• *One day Jesus was praying in a certain place. When he finished, one of his disciples said to him, 'Lord, teach us to pray, just as John taught his disciples'.*

He said to them, 'When you pray, say: "Father, hallowed be your name, your kingdom come, give us each day our daily bread.

Forgive us our sins, for we also forgive everyone who sins against us, and lead us not into temptation." •• *(LK 11:1-13)*

LECTIO DIVINA – or godly reading, is used by many people to help them to pray. You may wish to slowly read and reflect on this prayer, line by line, firstly by reading slowly and stopping to reflect.

Then, noticing which word or phrase seems to draw you today, let that sink in to a deeper level within your heart and savour it, as though 'tasting' it.

Finally, speak to God from your heart or simply remain in silence, aware of the presence of our God who loves us with a parent's love, feeding us as Jesus fed the multitude, curing our ills as he did, and drawing us closer to the profound holiness of God.

Where even two or three
are gathered in my name

there I truly am among them.

Where even two or three are gathered in my name,
    there I am in the midst of them.
Where even two or three are gathered in my name,
    there I truly am among them.

And the gift that I am bringing is the power
    that has touched your time,
    the light before your eyes I am,
    and the Kingdom I am bringing is not made with gold;
    it can't be bought or sold
    yet can be surely found.
And the bread that I am giving
    is the gift of life that cannot end
    broken till the world is healed again.

Where even two or three are gathered in my name,
    there I truly am among them.

It can be surely seen, this Kingdom that I bring,
    it can be surely found
    where even two or three are gathered in my name
    there I am in the midst of them.
Where even two or three are gathered in my name,
    there I truly am among them.

Tom McGuinness sj

there I truly am among them

46

To walk humbly with your God

As we now understand what is, perhaps, the most profound meaning of the painting, one cannot look at the feet of the younger son without wondering about his journey, not merely the journey home, but all the wandering and squandering that have characterised his misspent youth. These are the feet of one who has suffered much on life's pilgrimage. It is not too difficult to imagine some of the hardships of the journey and to travel on the same road with him.

These are the feet his mother tickled when she washed them. These feet played happily on his father's farm, chasing playmates and dreams. They rode away, richly shod when, as a young man, he was bent on seeing the world, and now they return, torn and bleeding, trudging wearily towards the familiar landscape of his childhood home. Rembrandt has created a strange harmony between the rags the young man wears and his bare feet. We can feel the sensitivity of the artist, above all, in his portrayal of the feet and hands in this picture, the bent posture of one who has been, quite literally, brought to his knees.

prayer – the journey of life

☐ *Whose feet are these, in any case? It is not difficult to see in them a symbol of the feet of the Saviour as he makes his final ascent to Jerusalem. They may also be your own feet on the journey through life. They are surely the feet of so many migrants in our world today. How much do you know about the world's refugee problem? Many Christian aid agencies will supply information.*

☐ *On a personal level, you may find yourself praying about your own life-journey and where your own feet have taken you in the recent past. Can you recognise God's touch along the way?*

scripture

•• *This is what the LORD says, 'Stand by the road and look. Ask for the ancient paths and know where the good way is. Walk on it and experience peace for yourselves.* •• (Jer 6:16)

•• *You have been told what is good and what the LORD requires of you: to do justice, to love tenderly, and to walk humbly with your God.* •• (Mic 6:8)

•• *I will lead the blind by ways which they do not know; along unseen paths I will guide them. I will turn darkness into light before them and make the rough ground smooth. These are the things that I will do, and I will not forsake them.* •• (Is 42:16)

I have carved you on the palms of my hands

The father, reaching out loving hands to his son, reveals what is probably one of the most astonishing features in any western painting. The hands that draw him close are not a pair. They represent all that can be uttered about human existence and, at the same time, they plumb profound depths about the truth of our God.

They lie on the shoulders of the son like the light yoke that Jesus describes as his own. They are both male and female at the same time. The hand on our right, the father's left hand, is a masculine hand and the hand of a labourer, perhaps the God who created all and holds everything in being. The right hand is a feminine hand and may represent the mothering and nurturing of a God who brings us to birth and touches our hearts with tenderness.

They remind us of the words of the letter to the Ephesians as they try to describe God... 'and then, you will have strength to grasp the breadth and the length, the height and the depth, so that you may be filled with the utter fullness of God' *(Eph 3:18-19)*.

You may wish to dwell, in prayer, on the different qualities that these hands represent. One is sinewy and work-torn, with dirty, broken nails and a muscular wrist and thumb. The other is more delicate with long, sensitive fingers, a narrow wrist and well-manicured nails. Masculine/feminine is not the only interpretation. First/third world may also spring to mind as some nations struggle for dignity and justice.

prayer

You may wish to look at your own hands and feet as you make this prayer, aware that each one is called to be God's daughter or son, the beloved child of God's heart. We, too, shall one day hear those words addressed to us, 'You are my child, the beloved. My favour rests on you' (Lk 3:22).

There are many opportunities for group or personal prayer and involvement. This prayer attributed to St Teresa of Avila may help you to pray.

Christ has no body now on earth but yours,
> no hands but yours,
> no feet but yours.
Yours are the eyes through which
> Christ's compassion is to look out to the world.
Yours are the feet by which he is to go about doing good.
And yours are the hands by which he is to bless us now.

scripture

Just as I was saying, 'The Lord has abandoned me; the Lord has forgotten me'.
Does a woman forget her baby, or fail to cherish the child of her womb?

Yet, even if these forget, I will never forget you. I have written your name on the palms of my hands. (Is 49:15-16)

Then he took the children in his arms and laying his hands on them, blessed them. (Mk 10:16)

Like a weaned child in his mother's arms... *Psalm 131*

Beyond, in the darkness that encloses the intimate moment of the father's embrace, Rembrandt has traced the figures of two women hovering at the edge of the scene. They gravitate towards the light that the artist has created to symbolise the greater light of God's presence. One is at an upper window and she appears to be looking down on the scene.

The other woman is closer. She hovers in the background, leaning against a pillar or arch that echoes the posture of the father's gently bending form. In this woman we may wish to imagine the mother of the Prodigal Son, standing in awe at the return of her lost child. She speaks to us of the intimacy of ordinary life, the daily tasks faithfully continued, despite the grief, then interrupted by a momentous arrival. She, too, has waited many years for her son's return, but she does not break into the heart-stirring moment of the father's embrace. Like the Spirit of God, she waits for the appropriate moment to enter the scene as she hovers in the shadows.

We struggle to find images of God, but one image that Jesus himself uses is that of a woman who, having lost a coin, sweeps the house until she finds it. He compares her to the Kingdom, or reign of God, who seeks the lost *(Lk 15:8-10)*. Elsewhere he compares the Kingdom to a baker woman who takes some yeast, mixes it with the flour, and leavens her dough until all of it is raised, ready for the oven *(Mt 13:33)*. What homely passages these are! Jesus also longs to gather the city of Jerusalem about him, as a mother hen gathers her chicks. By Jerusalem we understand all those he wishes to save: his own people and the nations of the world, creating Jerusalem anew in the Spirit *(Mt 23:37-39)*.

So Jesus presents us with these images of a loving, parenting God who can be described as father and mother to us. In the Hebrew testament there is a body of literature known as the Wisdom literature. It parallels other traditions in scripture, like the Prophets, and it gives us unique insights into the being of God. Jesus would have prayed and studied in this tradition which recognises those particular, 'mothering', qualities we find in God. For example, he would have prayed the words of the psalmist, 'Like a weaned child on its mother's breast, even so is my soul' *(Ps 131:2)*. When he prayed those words, perhaps he brought to mind the times that he spent in Mary's arms when he was a small child.

prayer

The Prodigal Son is gathered into the 'mothering' arms of God and Rembrandt chooses to place women at the scene and seek them out with his brush strokes. We may wish to stand with them, gently looking on, listening to the murmured words and seeing the tender gestures, safe in the shadow of our God.

scripture

•• O Lord, my heart is not proud nor do I have arrogant eyes.

I am not engrossed in ambitious matters, nor in things too great for me.

I have quieted and stilled my soul like a weaned child on its mother's lap;

like a contented child is my soul.

Hope in the Lord, O Israel, now and forever. •• (Ps 131)

Make your home in me

We return now to the contemplation of the whole painting as our prayer moves to that place deep within us where we encounter God.

In the sombre darkness, the figures glow before us like an eternal hearth. From the darkness without, all are drawn to the warmth and safety of this hearth, with the elder son, the bystanders, the Prodigal Son's mother, looking on at a distance.

Now step close to the hearth that is God's own self. It is a homecoming for each one of us. Warm yourself at the fire of God's love. Gaze at the flames and their flickering light. Be mindful of the presence of God with the Hebrew people in the desert, in the form of a pillar of fire by night. When the night seems to overwhelm us we can gaze within and seek out the fire that is in our hearts. The generosity of the Father's forgiveness and reconciliation glow like embers within us. We wait for them to be fanned into a flame by the breath of God's Holy Spirit. As we wait, we are filled with gratitude at this mystery of transformation which Rembrandt has captured for us.

We remember that the Paschal mystery is played out before us in this parable and painting. Now we move to the wonder of Pentecost and the unity that is foreshadowed there as the disciples perceive the flames leaping about them. We are told that they were filled with the Holy Spirit. Fear is banished and they are able to communicate across barriers of language and race.

prayer

St John of the Cross describes God's being as a 'living flame of love'. He describes the burning light of God as a lamp which reveals the deepest recesses of the heart (cf The Living Flame of Love *by John of the Cross). We have no need to fear this scrutiny. When God's Spirit came among the disciples it was characterised by rich gifts and deep graces. Unity was visible across the barriers of race, language and status. St Paul describes for us the gifts of the Spirit in his first letter to the Corinthians (cf 12:4-11 ff).*

> O Lamps of fire!
> In whose splendours
> The deep caverns of feeling,
> Once obscure and blind,
> Now give forth, so rarely, so exquisitely,
> both warmth and light to the Beloved.
>
> *(John of the Cross, The Living Flame of Love, Stanza 3)*

scripture

I will pour out my Spirit on every mortal.
Your sons and daughters will prophesy,
your old will dream dreams, your young will see visions.
Even upon my servants and maidens, I will pour out my Spirit on that day...
Then all who call upon the name of the Lord will be saved. (JOEL 3: 1-5)

Suddenly there came from heaven the sound, as it were, of a mighty wind, that filled the entire house and there appeared to them tongues of fire; these separated and came to rest on the head of each of them. They were filled with the Holy Spirit. (ACTS 2:1-4)

61

...let the feast begin!